Power Before The Throne

Before The Throne

by Ruth Rieder

"In an age fraught with indecision and compromise, how refreshing to hear Bible truths so clearly proclaimed and in such an able manner. Sister Rieder lives, and now explains truths held near to the heart of God. Surely, 'Power Before The Throne' has '. . . Come to the Kingdom for such a time as this.'"

— Reverend Larry Booker,
Pastor & Conference Speaker

Power Before The Throne

Copyright © 1999
Ruth Rieder

ALL RIGHTS RESERVED
No portion of this publication may be reproduced, stored in any electronic system, or transmitted in any form or by any means, electronic, mechanical, photocopy, recording, or otherwise, without written permission from the author. Brief quotations may be used in literary reviews.

All artwork drawn by Wade Plemons

Unless otherwise indicated, all Scripture quotations are taken from the King James Version of the Bible.

FOR INFORMATION CONTACT:
Ruth Rieder
P. O. Box 15252
Rio Rancho, NM 87174
ISBN: 0-7392-0121-2

Printed in the USA by

MORRIS PUBLISHING

3212 East Highway 30 • Kearney, NE 68847 • 1-800-650-7888

I dedicate these writings to my precious daughters, Angelica Grace and Miriam Hope.

May they have a revelation of true holiness and be joyful in obedience to their Lord. May they also be diligent "guardians of the glory" and never abdicate their "power before the throne." My prayer is that they never stray from the pathway of righteousness and that they would dance on the streets of gold with us and with those who have gone before and blazed a trail of righteousness.

Acknowledgments

I thank my Lord and Master Jesus Christ for giving me an understanding into His Word. Thank you for providing the finances to print this book. I love you more than anything else in this world. You are my life, my first love and my consuming desire! May my life praise you.

MY BELOVED HUSBAND: Thank you for your wise and understanding ways, for believing in me and supporting me 100%. Thank you for being a "Word Warrior" and encouraging me in my pursuit of God through His Word. I love you, darling!

Sis. Oakes: Thank you for being the catalyst to cause me to embark on this endeavor. You are a true friend, and your friendship has greatly enriched my life.

Wade Plemons: Thank you for the anointed and superb artwork.

Sis. Donna Ten Eyck and my Armor Bearers: Thank

you for your prayer covering and for being laborers together with me. Sis. Donna, you have been that friend I needed so often. Thank you for your hours of work and assistance in the fine tuning of this manuscript. You have lightened my load.

Sis. Joan Pierce: Thank you for your wise counsel and editing that enhanced the readability of this book.

Sis. Bethany Sledge: Thank you for your excellent work in the formatting and proofreading of this manuscript.

Sis. LaJoyce Martin and Sis. Pauline Johnson: Thank you for your guidance and invaluable information.

I am deeply grateful for my praying "German Shepherd" father, the late Rev. L. Wm. Schmidt. Thank you, Dad, for all you invested in my life. I give honor to my godly mother. She is a true example of holiness, and I rise up to call her "blessed." Thank you, Mom and Dad, for instilling in me the fear of the Lord and for bringing me up in a home where Jesus came first.

Table of Contents

Foreword 11

Introduction 13

Chapter One:
    Revelation Or Perish! 15

Chapter Two:
    Role Reversal vs. God's Order 21

Chapter Three:
    The Million Dollar Question 35

Chapter Four:
    Who Really Is In Bondage? 41

Chapter Five:
    We Have No Such Custom! 49

Chapter Six:
    Guardians Of The Glory 55

Chapter Seven:
    Power Before The Throne 81

Foreword

It is encouraging to see the next generation of Pentecost willing to carry the torch into the new millennium. It is obvious that Sis. Ruth Rieder, pastor's wife, Texico District Women's Division President, National Coordinator for Daughters of Zion, and mother of two daughters, is passionate about living for God and is unafraid to take a stand for our Bible-based positions of separation from a world gone out of control.

Here is a book for those who want to live their lives in full harmony with the will and Word of God, a book that is personal, convincing, and scriptural. I pray that it will trigger in you a gentle explosion or maybe a total revolution. We must possess a single-minded passion to please God and to offer the members of our bodies for His service.

Obeying Christ delivers us from our fatal tendency

to self-will and creates in us the true spirit of self-surrender. To obey Him in these matters will cause us to serve the Lord with gladness because we have seen His glory and are satisfied indeed.

When you finish this book, you will have a clear understanding concerning some of the most controversial subjects that confront women. Most importantly, you will have the peace of mind that comes from understanding a clear-cut truth. This book will enable us to be rapture ready with Power Before The Throne!

— Gwyn Oakes, Women's Division President of the United Pentecostal Church, International

Introduction

In these last days, we are waging a war concerning the essentiality of holiness. Holiness standards are being used to bring confusion to the Body of Christ, and women are especially targeted. One of the strongest areas of perplexity is the significance of hair length. The time has come to expose our enemy's tactics. We need strong preachers of righteousness who will fearlessly declare the whole counsel of God.

Proverbs 15:14 says, *"The heart of him that hath understanding seeketh knowledge: but the mouth of fools feedeth on foolishness."* There are men and women of God seeking for understanding concerning the matter of holiness. Each time I have spoken on this topic, I have been literally overwhelmed by the response it has elicited. I have been urged by my elders to put into print the special insight the Lord has afforded to me while I sought out this subject. The very day that I sat down to write this book, I received a phone call from Illinois entreating me for material on this subject. God is clearly issuing a call to His church to *"stand ye in the ways, and see, and ask for the old paths, where is the good way, and walk therein, and ye shall find rest for your souls"* (Jeremiah 6:16). May the last half of this verse never apply to any of us, *"But they said, We will not walk therein."* According to Luke 8:15, the good and honest heart hears the Word and keeps it. James 1:21 tells us to *"receive with meekness the engrafted word, which is able to save your souls."* Your response to the Word of God will determine your destiny.

My prayer is that this book will provide Biblical answers and understanding to the young and old alike and will be a useful tool in the hands of the Church. May we learn to delight in being holy unto our Lord, joyfully dancing on the Highway of Holiness all the way to the New Jerusalem!

Revelation Or Perish!

During a recent Ladies Conference in which we discussed the holiness issues that confront us, one sister said, "I've always been obedient to holiness because I love the Lord." That is a right and noble reason and is, of course, the true foundation for all obedience. *"For this is the love of God, that we keep his commandments: and his commandments are not grievous"* (I John 5:3).

When we love Him, no price will be too great to pay to please Him and see Him face to face. When we love Him, we are willing to forsake all to follow Him. My dear grandfather, the late A. D. Urshan, admonished my mother Faith that if she would just fall in love with Jesus, it would be easy to obey and serve Him.

We need a good, old-fashioned dose of the "fear of

the Lord" coupled with our love for God. When we fear Him, we will not want to displease Him. Our love for Him will cause us to do everything in our power to walk worthy unto all pleasing. Then like Psalm 25:14 promises, He will whisper His secrets in our ears, and we will have ears to hear what the Spirit saith unto the Church. He will not whisper His secrets into the ears of those that will mock and desecrate them. However, He will reveal His covenant to those that love Him and will give them an understanding or revelation into His Word. When He gives us revelation, then we will not perish. If we love the Lord with all our heart, mind, soul, and strength, obedience to Him will become our number one priority.

It is deeply disturbing to watch as friends and fellow ministers cast off former holiness convictions and talk about this life and law of liberty they now enjoy. The landmarks erected by our forefathers are dismissed as unnecessary. We see how those who once embraced a life of holiness now deem it "old-fashioned" and out of touch. "After all, this is a different era. We live in a high tech society, and if we would just loosen up a little, then we could identify more fully with the world that we are trying to reach." That is the common theme threaded throughout the argument they set forth. This satanic falsehood is cloaked under the deceiving guise of compassion and a supposed desire to win more souls. "Why, just look at how we can impact this world for Christ," is the message that is parroted. They are bold in their newfound "liberties" and chide us for being so behind the times.

Those who hold fast to the ancient landmarks have been labeled as legalists and pharisaical. However, the voice of the Spirit is calling us to a deeper understanding of God's requirements. We must be on guard against any voices that would tell us to loosen up and cast off the restraints of separation from the world. God has never wanted His people to blend in with the world around them. He has always been a God of separation throughout the Old and New Testaments. The Apostle Paul warns us of this in Philippians 3:17-20, ***"Brethren, be followers together of me, and mark them which walk so as ye have us for an example. (For many walk, of whom I have told you often, and now tell you even weeping, that they are the enemies of the cross of Christ: Whose end is destruction, whose God is their belly, and whose glory is in their shame, <u>who</u>***

mind earthly things.) For our conversation is in heaven; from whence also we look for the Saviour, the Lord Jesus Christ." Let us walk as Paul walked and mark those who walk in the same manner, keeping company with them.

Beware of those who glory in returning to the vomit of this world and wallowing in the filth that the Lord washed them from with His own precious blood. This will not bring liberty. Instead, it results in being entangled once again by the bondage of this world. To justify such decisions, they fool themselves by glorying in their shame– the shame of losing the covering of God's holiness and putting on the gaudy substitutes and ugly version of the world's beauty. They brazenly flaunt their newfound "freedoms" (see II Peter 2), but our conversation or behavior is in heaven. We must not get caught up in minding earthly things and indulging our fleshly appetites for fame and fortune. In addition to love for God and the fear of the Lord, we need one more ingredient that will aid us in our obedience. **Revelation!**

"Where there is no vision, the people perish: but he that keepeth the law, happy is he" (Proverbs 29:18).

For many years this Scripture has been used to

Revelation Or Perish!

describe how the Church needed a vision, encompassing a corporate and individual vision on every level. We were told that unless we had a vision, our church would go nowhere. This is true; however, this interpretation only encompasses the beginning portion of this Scripture. An in-depth examination of the complete verse helps to open our understanding to a very important spiritual principle. The word "vision" in the Hebrew language is the word **chazown** (pronounced *khaw-' zone*), meaning "revelation." The word "perish" is the Hebrew word **para** (pronounced *paw-'rah*), meaning "to loosen; dismiss; avoid; absolve, go back, make naked; to bare; **uncover;** to set at naught, (cast off restraints)."

We need to be able to give answers to the new converts, and it is imperative that we are equipped to teach it clearly to subsequent generations. The revelation must be passed on, or with each succeeding decade, our descendants will begin to loosen up. The landmarks will be dismissed as unimportant. The sacred precepts that God requires of us will be set at naught. Slowly they will begin to wend their way back to Egypt and be made naked. The commandments they deem unnecessary will be avoided.

They will absolve or be set free from the obligation of obedience and resultant consequences of guilt. The tragic culmination of these choices will lift the protective covering of holiness and cause them to be exposed to the destruction of disobedience as they begin to flippantly cast off restraints.

The NIV translation states, ***"Where there is no revelation, the people cast off restraint; but blessed is he who keeps the law."*** Now, the second portion of this verse, which focuses on the blessedness of obedience, fits with the beginning.

WE MUST HAVE REVELATION, OR WE WILL PERISH!

Role Reversal vs. God's Order

Apostle Paul said to be a follower of him and also to follow him as he follows Christ. Let us examine Paul's teachings in order to understand the path we are to walk. In I Corinthians 11:3, Paul lays out God's order and line of authority for the Church. It is as follows:

- **GOD (Spirit)**
- **CHRIST (the Sonship–the man Christ Jesus, in submission to God the Father)**
- **MAN**
- **WOMAN**

You might start a riot in the workplace if you talk about

this order of submission. One day while on the job, a woman asked my sister Beth why she didn't cut her hair. Beth said that it was a sign of submission to her husband, to which the woman replied, "I know one thing; I'll never be a Pentecostal!" The rebellious spirit of our age was manifesting itself in all of its power.

Headship and submission do not imply superiority and inferiority but rather responsibility and relationship. The husband is the head of the wife in the sense that he is responsible for her protection, her provision, and her guidance (Ephesians 5:23,25-28,31,33 and I Peter 3:7). God never intended for the husband to treat the wife as an inferior slave or a doormat under his feet. He is to love and cherish her as Christ does the Church.

A wife is to allow her husband to fulfill his role, submitting to his loving, sacrificial leadership as the church submits to Christ. Ephesians 5:22,24,33 and I Peter 3:1,5-6 explain what the woman's response should be to her husband's leadership. Women are not inferior to their husbands, but they do have a different role. Husbands and wives work together for a beautiful home.

God established an order in I Corinthians 11, and our

Role Reversal vs. God's Order

hair symbolizes our position in that order. *"Every man praying or prophesying, having his head covered, dishonoureth his head"* (I Corinthians 11:4). When a man allows his hair to grow long, he dishonors Christ, who is his head. When a man prays or prophesies with an uncovered head or short hair, he is demonstrating his submission to Christ.

"But every woman that prayeth or prophesieth with her head uncovered dishonoureth her head: for that is even all one as if she were shaven" (I Corinthians 11:5). The woman demonstrates her submission to her head by a covered head or long hair. If a woman is unmarried, her head would be her male leader–her dad, guardian, or pastor. Since this pertains to how we come before the presence of God, then we must practice it at all times. Paul said in I Thessalonians 5:17 to *"Pray without ceasing,"* and Jesus said in Luke 18:1, *"Men ought always to pray."* Paul also stated in Acts 17:28, *"For in him we live, and move, and have our being...."* I Corinthians 11:15 gives a proper definition of the covering that is in question, *"for her hair is given her for a covering."* It is the hair and not a hat or a veil. A woman cannot pray, cut her hair, and

then six months later pray again. We need a lifestyle of obedience.

"For if the woman be not covered, let her also be shorn: but if it be a shame for a woman to be shorn or shaven, let her be covered" (I Corinthians 11:6). Let us look at four important definitions:

- **SHAVE:** to remove the beard or other body hair with a razor or shaver. If you are talking about a shaved head, it is a nude head!
- **SHORN:** past participle of shear. What does shear make you think of? Sheep.
- **SHEAR:** to remove hair by clipping or cutting. To cut or clip with a sharp instrument. There is no mention of a specified amount (small or large, etc.) that is being removed by this process.
- **TRIM:** an act of cutting or to remove by cutting. Very same thing as cut, no difference. Again, there is no mention made of the amount being trimmed. It could be a small or large amount as well.

Role Reversal vs. God's Order

When God tells a woman not to cut her hair in the context of God's order and she rebels by cutting her hair, she then assumes the position of the man, who is commanded by God to show his submission through an uncovered head or cut hair. In so doing, she usurps the position of the man and is out of her position in God's order. As God's Church, we are to maintain the order set forth from the creation.

If a woman is going to trim her hair, she might as well shear it all off. In fact, shave it off. It's one and the same if it is shaved, cut, or trimmed. How much she removes does not make any difference because God is looking at the woman, and He knows that she is out of her place in the order of creation.

Looking again at I Corinthians 11:6, the Word admonishes us that whether a woman cuts, trims, shears, or is shaven, it is a shame. *"For if the woman be not covered, let her also be shorn: but if it be a shame for a woman to be shorn or shaven, let her be covered."* What word in this verse causes you to realize it is wrong to cut your hair? It is the word **SHAME!** It is a shame no matter how much is removed! We are not talking about a little wagging of the finger and saying, "Shame on you." Jude 13 says, *"Raging waves of the sea, foaming out their own shame; wandering stars, to whom is reserved the blackness of darkness for ever."* DOING THINGS THAT ARE A SHAME CAN SEND YOU TO HELL!

SOME THINGS THAT ARE A SHAME IN THE BIBLE:

- LYING (Proverbs 13:5)
- RAPE (II Samuel 13:13)
- FOLLY (Deuteronomy 22:21, Proverbs 3:35, Proverbs 18:13)
- PRIDE (Proverbs 11:2)
- STUBBORNNESS (Judges 2:19, Proverbs 13:18, Jeremiah 3:25)
- NAKEDNESS (Exodus 32:25, Isaiah 47:3, Revelation 3:18, Revelation 16:15)
- LUST (Hosea 4:18, Nahum 3:4-6; see these Scriptures in the NIV Bible translation)
- IDOLATRY (Jeremiah 13:26-27, Ezekiel 16:52-54, Ezekiel 44:12-13)

Role Reversal vs. God's Order

Are any of these a sin? Ladies, cutting your hair in any amount falls into the same category of shame.

A shaved head was an obvious mark of shame in the Scriptures. Deuteronomy 21:10-14 bears this out. It was part of the humiliation process for the captives. It's a shame in our society as well. It was used to humiliate the Jewish women during WWII. What do women do who lose their hair because of sickness or a disease? They respond by covering up with a hat, a scarf, or a wig.

"For a man indeed ought not to cover his head, forasmuch as he is the image and glory of God: but the woman is the glory of the man" (I Corinthians 11:7). Why is it that we believe men should cut their hair, but women do not need to leave theirs uncut? Or why is it so laughable to think of a man in a skirt, but it is okay for women to wear pants? In essence we are saying the man has to submit to God's law, but the woman is exempt from obedience. FOOD FOR THOUGHT!

This Scripture says that the woman is the glory of the man. Glory means: "a highly praiseworthy or brilliant asset; something that secures praise or renown; resplendence, magnificence." Wives are the resplendent, majestic beauty of their husbands. She is an asset to him that secures praise and brings honor to him. The actions of a woman can make or break a good man. Proverbs 12:4 tells us, *"A virtuous woman is a crown to her husband: but she that maketh ashamed is as rottenness in his bones."* A crown is a symbol of authority, majesty, and glory. Paul uses two contrasting words, shame and glory, to describe the consequences of our actions. Cut hair on a woman shows a rejection of authority and brings shame while uncut hair is a recognizable attribute of a glorious and honorable woman. The cutting of a woman's hair is an **outward symptom of an inward condition called lack of submission.**

"Judge in yourselves: is it comely that a woman pray unto God uncovered? Doth not even nature itself teach you, that, if a man have long hair, it is a shame unto him?" (I Corinthians 11:13-14). The Full Life Study Bible has an interesting commentary on this Scripture. It states: "In N.T. times, long hair was disgraceful and shunned by Jewish men as well as by those in first century Corinth. Pictures portraying Jesus as having long hair are based wholly on the imagination of the artists from the

Role Reversal vs. God's Order

Middle Ages, not on Biblical or historical evidence (thousands of paintings and sculptures from N.T. times prove this). The apostle would not have written, 'if a man have long hair, it is a shame unto him,' if Jesus had worn his hair long as did women. Hence, Paul's statement is in conflict not with the custom of Jesus, but with the invention of artists." Paul felt that the Corinthians were capable of judging whether or not it was appropriate for a woman to pray to God uncovered on the basis of nature. God has placed that sense of propriety in us from the beginning, but the rebellion in our society is drowning it out.

One Sunday morning on the way to church, my two girls were playing with their Barbie and Ken dolls. As I looked at the dolls, I began to realize that our society is without excuse. The Barbie dolls all had long hair, and the Ken dolls all had short hair. Deep down inside, people still know what is right. When they stand before God and proclaim ignorance of His law, all He has to do is to show them the dolls that they created. I wonder if we'll ever see Ken with a ponytail and Barbie with a butch hair cut? The long hair on men and short hair on women is a clear indication that our society is totally out of God's creation order.

A rather humorous incident which clearly illustrates role reversal happened to us one day while on an outing to the local zoo. My mother and I were on our way into the ladies' restroom when, to our amazement, what appeared to be a man was walking in there in front of us. This individual was dressed in blue jeans, a manly looking short-sleeved shirt and had close-cropped, dark hair. Even the deportment of this person was very masculine. My mother rushed to this individual to inform him that this was the women's restroom. Looking down, this person who was masculine in dress, demeanor, and looks proceeded to let my mother know that she was a woman. You surely couldn't have told by looking at her.

Our society is in role reversal like never before. The men look like women with their long hair, earrings, and feminine ways while the women parade around with their lopped off hair and masculine clothes. Deuteronomy 22:5 emphatically tells us, *"The woman shall not wear that which pertaineth unto a man, neither shall a man put on a woman's garment: for all that do so are abomination unto the LORD thy God."* The reason this is so abominable

Role Reversal vs. God's Order

to God is that it is an outward indication of the role reversal that is rampant today. If it was an abomination to God in the Old Testament, it is still an abomination in the New Testament. Abominations to mankind may change, but abominations to God never change.

Here are some other things that are an abomination to God:

- HUMAN SACRIFICE (Deuteronomy 12:31)
- HOMOSEXUALITY (Leviticus 18:22,20:13)
- IDOLATRY (Deuteronomy 7:25-26,13:12-18, 27:15)
- BLEMISHED SACRIFICES (Deuteronomy 17:1)
- WITCHCRAFT (Deuteronomy 18:9-14)
- UNJUST WEIGHTS AND BALANCES (Deuteronomy 25:13-16, Proverbs 11:1,20:23)
- A PROUD LOOK (Proverbs 6:16-17)
- A LYING TONGUE (Proverbs 6:16-17)
- HANDS THAT SHED INNOCENT BLOOD (Proverbs 6:16-17)
- AN HEART THAT DEVISETH WICKED

IMAGINATIONS (Proverbs 6:16-18)
- FEET THAT BE SWIFT IN RUNNING TO MISCHIEF (Proverbs 6:16-18)
- A FALSE WITNESS THAT SPEAKETH LIES (Proverbs 6:16-19)
- HE THAT SOWETH DISCORD AMONG BRETHREN (Proverbs 6:16-19)

Working abomination in the sight of God can bar you from the New Jerusalem. It can blot out your name from the Lamb's book of life. *"And there shall in no wise enter into it any thing that defileth, <u>neither whatsoever worketh abomination</u>, or maketh a lie: but they which are written in the Lamb's book of life"* (Revelation 21:27). We are talking serious business!

Wearing clothes that pertain to the opposite sex falls into the same category as these other perverted sins mentioned above. The wearing of pants is another reflection of the role reversal in our world. Women began to wear pants openly and without censure during WWII when they took on a man's role in the factories. To do a man's job, they began to wear men's clothing, and it became an acceptable

Role Reversal vs. God's Order

practice to wear them all the time.

Isaiah 14:12-14 tells about the greatest attempt at role reversal that has ever taken place. Lucifer was the son of the morning, the anointed cherub that covereth, but he was not content with the role that God had ordained for him. He attempted to stage a role reversal with God and to usurp God's authority. He said, *"I will ascend into heaven, I will exalt my throne above the stars of God: I will sit also upon the mount of the congregation, in the sides of the north: I will ascend above the heights of the clouds; I will be like the most High."* Of course, he was no match for El Shaddai, the Almighty. He was cast out of heaven, but his tactic has never changed. That is what humanism is all about. Mankind is trying to stage a role reversal with God by proclaiming that they are their own gods.

Is it not interesting that restroom signs are universal all over the world? The woman is wearing a dress, and the man is wearing pants. The world understands perfectly what these symbols mean. I remember hearing Bro. Huntley preach about his daughter's response to the kids in school who pestered her about why she wore dresses. She asked them to draw a stick man and then a stick woman. She pointed to the stick woman who was identified by her skirt, and she told them, "That is why I wear dresses. I'm a girl!"

The world will be without excuse when they stand before God. When it comes to the matter of dress and the distinction of the sexes, all He will have to do is show them their restroom signs or ask them to draw a stick man and woman.

Our hair and our dress are an outward sign of our inward condition. We are either occupying our place in God's order, or we are trying to stage a role reversal.

The Million Dollar Question: How Long Is Long?

Just because a woman has hair that is long in length does not mean that she is being obedient to the ordinance of God set forth in I Corinthians 11. So, how long is long? To answer this question correctly, we need to have an understanding of what Paul is actually saying in the Greek language. We find our answer in the two words that Paul used concerning hair.

The first word is **komao** (pronounced *kom-'ah-o*), a verb. **Komao** is translated "have long hair" in I Corinthians 11:14-15. According to *Gingrich's Lexicon*, the word is defined as "wear long hair, to let one's hair grow long." *Thayer's Lexicon* has the same essential meaning.

It says, "let the hair grow, have long hair." If you trim or cut your hair to keep it at a certain length, you obviously are not letting it grow. It is impossible to grow your hair and yet cut it at the same time.

The second word is **kome** (pronounced '*kom-ay*), a noun. The use of the word **kome** also gives us a clear indication as to what Paul meant when he wrote this passage. This is the word that is translated "hair" in verse 15 where it says "for her hair [or her 'kome'] is given her for a covering." Two reference works in particular, *Bauer's Lexicon* and Moulton and Milligan's *Vocabulary of the Greek New Testament* both attest to the fact that "kome" demands the meaning of uncut hair. It is used to describe uncut hair in Greek literature, and it describes the Nazarites who were commanded not to cut their hair.

We refer back to our question of "How long is long?" In light of the meaning of these two words, the issue is not long or short hair but is **UNCUT** hair. Each of our scalps was made to hold a certain amount of hair. That is why some hair grows to the ankles and other hair only grows to the shoulders. Our physical makeup and the genes that we inherited from our parents affect the length

The Million Dollar Question

of our hair. If there were a specific length that we all had to conform to, then God would have had to lay it out in His Word so that we could be sure that we were being obedient to Him.

Just imagine if your pastor's wife had to have a tape measure to calculate the length of your hair so that she could verify that you were measuring up to what God required before you could be used in the ministry of your church. Such an idea is ludicrous! Some of us would never have a chance to pass this supreme test and would always be on the wrong side in this matter through no fault of our own. Can you see what a state of confusion this would create in the Church? The only way that we can all be on equal footing before the Lord in this requirement is if the definition of long is **UNCUT**!

You can have hair down to your knees, but if you trim it, your hair is not long according to God's standards. Your hair may only reach to your shoulders, but if it is uncut, in God's eyes it is long. If you've been cutting or trimming your hair and you want to regain your proper place in God's order, you must immediately put a stop to this practice of disobedience in your life. You must repent and refuse to continue to rebel against the Lord's requirements. What is more important to you–the vanity of your appearance or obedience to your Lord?

Some may have a personal conviction concerning the wearing of the veil or a second covering. The Bible plainly states in verse 15 that **"her hair is given her for a covering."** The word "for" is the Greek word **ante** which means "instead of." So our hair is given to us *for* or instead of (ante) a covering. Our hair is God-made. A veil is man-made. If you feel it is necessary to wear a veil or this is what your pastor teaches, by all means adhere to your convictions and obey your pastor. However, do not cut or trim the covering that was provided by God Himself, for this will place you in disobedience to God's command. As you read further in this book, you will see the dire consequences that this can bring upon you and your family.

Now, to answer our "Million Dollar Question" of "How long is long?" Long hair is hair that is uncut, untouched by scissors or other sharp instruments of hair removal, including burning or any other means that the devious human mind can manufacture. Trying to skirt compliance with the law of God is the true definition of

The Million Dollar Question

legalism–trying to find loopholes.

Who Really Is In Bondage?

Is it possible to have the wrong covering? Let us look at Isaiah 30:1-2, which warns, *"Woe to the rebellious children, saith the LORD, that take counsel, but not of me; <u>and that cover with a covering, but not of my spirit</u>, that they may add sin to sin: That walk to go down into Egypt, and have not asked at my mouth; to strengthen themselves in the strength of Pharaoh, and to trust in the shadow of Egypt!"* Egypt throughout Scripture has always typified sin and the place of bondage. This earthly kingdom continually spews out its counsel by way of the media. Returning home after many years on the mission field, my sister, Beth, began to look at the women's magazines. She told me she felt ugly when she read them because of all the embellishments they prescribed that were necessary for beauty. She refused to be influenced by their counsel and would no longer purchase them.

The beauty of this world is a painted caricature compared to the true beauty of holiness. The most beautiful women in the entire world are the handmaidens of the Lord. We must take our counsel not from Egypt but from the New Jerusalem. Blessed is the one who walketh not in the counsel of the ungodly. If magazines influence you to walk down and try out the fashions of Egypt, you need to get rid of them and begin to look into the Book that is the mirror of holiness.

When the saints of God go into a city for a General Conference, people stand up and take notice. A minister friend tells of being on an elevator during one such meeting. He overheard two businessmen talking about all the lovely women with their beautiful hair and attractive clothing. These two men were amazed to see women who looked and acted like ladies. The world recognizes the beauty and elegance of God's people.

We should never hang our heads in shame. We are, as I Peter 2:9 says, *"a chosen generation, a royal priesthood, an holy nation, a peculiar people; that ye should shew forth the praises of him who hath called you out of darkness into his marvellous light."* The Greek word for "praises" in this verse is **arete** (pronounced *ar-'et-ay*), and it actually means "virtues." Virtue means: "conformity to a standard of right: morality; a particular moral excellence; active power to accomplish a given effect: potency, efficacy; chaste." So this Scripture passage is not talking about singing some praise choruses but about a lifestyle that shows forth the virtues of the One who hath called us out of the darkness of sin into His marvelous light.

How can we shine and be a beacon of light in this dark world if we look just like they do? We are to shine forth with the moral excellence of our Father as we conform to His standard of righteousness. God does not want a weak, worldly, watered down version of His Church in these last days. He wants a potent, powerful, and purposeful Church. A city set on a hill cannot be hid! We are to be that beacon of hope, a place of refuge to which the world can turn. We are identifiable as followers of Christ (Christians) if we are properly showing forth the virtues (praises) of God.

As we examine the teachings of Paul, he tells us in

II Corinthians 11:2, ***"For I am jealous over you with godly jealousy: for I have espoused you to one husband, that I may present you as a <u>chaste virgin</u> to Christ."*** God is looking for a **<u>chaste virgin</u>** who has kept herself unspotted from the world. He is not in the market for a painted harlot-looking bride, but He wants a bride who has been faithful to Him and has not defiled herself with the ways of Egypt.

The modern woman still uses a covering, but it is not the covering of the Spirit. They are shedding their hair and covering up with make-up. Their substitute for the long hair that God has ordained is the make-up kit. Instead of glorying in the appearance and recognition of long hair and a clean face, the world says we must glorify or beautify our appearance with a covering of make-up and other adornments. The glory of these things could never compare to the glory and beauty with which God adorns His bride. Their substitute is cheap and tawdry! We need to get our counsel from the Bible and not from Egypt's tabloids.

We have heard the advice they offer, "Well, if the barn needs painting, paint it." We are not barns! Psalm 144:12 likens our sons to living plants and our daughters to

Who Really Is In Bondage?

polished cornerstones of a palace. We do not paint our rose bushes or our pets. Have you ever been to the zoo and seen the zookeeper painting the elephants with pink and purple polka dots? We do not paint living things. If a builder constructed a lovely palace out of the finest marble, he would not dream of covering its beauty with a coat of cheap paint. Why do we think that we need the covering of Egypt? The beauty that God bestows is likened to the enduring splendor of a palace. However, the world tells us that we are like barns and that we can only find beauty in the peeling paint of make-up. The longer this paint is worn, the more it ages the skin. Take a look at older women in our society, and notice the way their appearance has been destroyed by chasing after the delusion of beauty that the world offers. Compare them to the graceful dignity of God's people whose hoary heads are found in the way of righteousness.

I would like you to consider another insult that Egypt heaps on women. They say that women need to paint themselves, but men do not. It is a wonder the feminist movement is not outraged by this blatant show of inequality. Men do not need paint, but we are barns and, therefore, do? Wake up! Do not swallow the falsehoods of this corrupt world system.

My husband, Michael, is the only member who is saved out of his family. Since I am a fourth generation Pentecostal, it has been an eye-opening experience to visit his family. One time we went to see his grandmother (JaJa) in California. We wanted to take JaJa out to lunch and give her a special treat. When my husband invited her, she promptly declined. Her excuse was that she did not have "her face on yet," and it would take too long to put it on. How many faces are you supposed to have? WHO REALLY IS IN BONDAGE? I can get dressed and go out every day without needing a secondary face. I have heard of women who will not even go out to the mailbox without their "face on." Paul tells us in Galatians 4:26, *"But Jerusalem which is above is free, which is the mother of us all."* We are born in the Church that is free and has made us free. We are free from the law of sin and death. If you are living in Egypt or have gone back to its borders, you are the one who is really in bondage. *"If the Son therefore shall make you free, ye shall be free indeed"* (John 8:36).

"So then, brethren, we are not children of the

Who Really Is In Bondage?

bondwoman, but of the free" (Galatians 4:31). We are not children of Hagar, the Egyptian bondmaid, but we are the children of promise.

One day while shopping in the mall with my family, I came upon a fashion display that was put together by a renowned encyclopedia company. It spotlighted the last one hundred years of fashion. Mannequins were dressed to show the development of the different fashions throughout the years. Each period of dress had an explanation accompanying it. We were quite interested to read that the fashions of the Roaring Twenties in which women began to rebel, cut off their hair, raise their hemlines, and wear make-up were a result of the discovery of King Tut's tomb. The women began to paint their faces and cut their hair to model themselves after the fashions of Egypt. It was all the rage. They even wore serpent headbands and bracelets like the slaves wore in Egypt. Does the scenario sound vaguely familiar–the serpent and the slavery? Once again mankind had been duped as they bit into the forbidden fruit, and the chains of slavery were tightened that much more. Paul exhorts us in Galatians 5:1 to **"*stand fast therefore in the liberty wherewith Christ hath made us***

***free,** and be not entangled again with the yoke of bondage."*

True liberty and freedom are only found in the Church of the living God. So, to answer the question, "Who really is in bondage?" the answer is loud and clear. It is those who have been taken captive by Egypt!

We Have No Such Custom!

"*But if any man seem to be contentious, we have no such custom, neither the churches of God*" (I Corinthians 11:16). To have a proper understanding of what Paul means in this verse, we need an understanding of the customs of that day. The National Geographic Magazine, June 1972, page 774, pictured an altar that was used for sacrificial offering of hair in Biblical times. It was found in the city of Aphrodeises, located in southwest Turkey. The temple of Aphrodite towered behind this blazing altar. The article said women entered to sacrifice their hair in annual mourning for the death of Aphrodite's lover, Adonis.

Young Greek maidens worshiped Diana as a major deity in the Grecian Empire. Her image was believed to have fallen down from Jupiter (Acts 19:35), and a magnificent temple was built to house this statue in the city of Ephesus. It was one of the Seven Wonders of the Ancient World.

The influence of this particular cult was very far-reaching. Even coins have been found with Diana's picture and the inscription "Diana Ephesis." Paul battled against it while ministering in Ephesus when Demetrius, a silversmith who made silver shrines for Diana, incited a riot in response to Paul's teachings. In earlier times, human sacrifice was also a part of their cultic worship; however, animals were protected, the hind being Diana's favorite beast. Eunuchs or emasculated men were used in the temple rites.

"In Biblical times when you entered Corinth, at the top of the hill was the temple of Diana. The first sailor from the sea to the top of the hill was given free access to the whole harlot harem of Diana. The prostitutes in the temple all had short hair. It had been given as a sacrifice to the goddess, Diana." (From the *Theological Dictionary of the New Testament* by Kittle and published by Urdman)

When the beautiful Greek maidens with their long,

We Have No Such Custom!

flowing hair came to prostitute themselves at the temple, they shaved off their long tresses of hair and cast them into the burning altar at the entryway of the temple as a sacrifice to Diana. "Young girls revered this goddess as guardian of their maiden years, and before marriage they offered her a lock of their hair, their girdle, and their maiden garment." (Excerpted from *Unger's Bible Dictionary*)

    The reason Paul took time to write I Corinthians 11 is because of the questions that were coming to him. He had to give answers to these new Christians in Greece. When these Greek women came to Jesus, this new God, they were assuming they should cut their hair in worship. They had done this type of thing for the gods they used to serve. That is why Paul had to write back and say in essence, "No, no, no. God gave you your hair for a covering, and 'if any man seem to be contentious, we have no such custom, neither the churches of God.'" He was saying we have no such custom in the Church of the living God as they have in the heathen temples or churches–that is, the custom of cutting or shaving off a woman's hair and offering it in sacrifice to a god or goddess.

Power Before The Throne

Our day and age are still in the same worship mode of female deities. No, we may not have a large physical temple erected that people can flock to, but the same spirit is alive and well. It is a temple of worship that masquerades under the guise of "Equal Rights, Women's Lib, and Feminism." Our society is no different from Paul's when you take away the cloak of seeming sophistication. Just as Diana was a guardian of the animals but demanded human sacrifice, so, too, our world advocates earth worship and values the rights of animals over the sanctity of human life. Babies are being sacrificed by the thousands every day on the altar of "a woman's right to choose."

This same evil spirit desires to rob men of their masculinity and proper leadership role while setting up the women as the authority figures. I heard a man say on a call-in radio show that all the problems in the world would be solved if women were at the head of every major country in the world. This is totally contrary to the Word of God, but such is the mind set of the world we live in. The spirit that the early Church faced is still alive and well today!

Jeremiah 7:29 declares, **"Cut off thine hair, O**

Jerusalem, and cast it away, and take up a lamentation on high places; for the LORD hath rejected and forsaken the generation of his wrath." This Scripture tells us that the cutting of your hair and casting it away is a sign of being forsaken by God. Why would we want to traffic in something that is a sign of being rejected by God?

In Jeremiah 7 when it speaks of cutting off your hair and casting it away as a sign of being forsaken by God, the preceding verses warn us that this came about because the people refused to hearken to the prophets that God sent to them. When they became disobedient, truth perished and was cut off from their mouth. The end result of their anarchy against God is described in verses 30-34. It is a mirror of what has happened in America as she has forgotten God. Children are being sacrificed, people are being murdered daily through random acts of violence, and our homes and marriages are being destroyed. *"The wicked shall be turned into hell, and all the nations that forget God"* (Psalm 9:17).

Jeremiah 7:30 says that the people of Judah have set up detestable idols in the house that bears His Name, defiling it. Paul emphatically declares in I Corinthians

6:19-20, *"What? know ye not that your body is the temple of the Holy Ghost which is in you, which ye have of God, and ye are not your own? For ye are bought with a price: therefore glorify God in your body, and in your spirit, which are God's."* God forbid that we would ever allow the idols of this world to be enshrined in a temple that bears His Name. I Peter 2:5 tells us, *"Ye also, as lively stones, are built up a spiritual house, an holy priesthood, to offer up spiritual sacrifices, acceptable to God by Jesus Christ."* The sacrifices of the wicked will never be permissible in a spiritual house, for they are an abomination to the Lord. We cannot embrace the customs of this world because James 4:4 tells us that friendship with the world is enmity with God. Their heathenish rites can never be incorporated into the worship that takes place in the temples that are inhabited by the Holy Ghost. *"We have no such custom, neither the churches of God!"*

Guardians Of The Glory

Ezekiel 28 offers some clues concerning the war that is being waged in the spirit realm over the matter of holiness. Lucifer had a very special place of anointed ministry, and his primary function was being the covering cherub. The cherubim, one of the angelic orders, seem to be particularly assigned the responsibility of guarding the glory of God. The verses that place them beside the throne of God and ever on guard are Psalm 80:1, Psalm 99:1, and Isaiah 37:16. Thus, Lucifer, as the anointed cherub, was set forth as the chief guardian of the glory of God. He carried out his duties before the Lord as he walked up and down in the midst of the stones of fire. Ezekiel 28:14 says that God put him in this place of delegated authority.

In light of such honor that was bestowed upon him

above all the other angels, what could possibly have been the root of his rebellion? What actually caused the iniquity to be birthed in his heart to the point of anarchy against God Almighty? Why would he revolt against his Creator? Ezekiel 28:17 gives us a very clear answer. It declares, **"Thine heart was lifted up because of thy beauty, thou hast corrupted thy wisdom by reason of thy brightness...."** Vanity caused him to become so proud of his outward magnificence that it began to overshadow his relationship with his Maker to the point of total rebellion. He was full of wisdom, but his wisdom was corrupted by reason of his brilliance. Turning traitor to the very glory that he was created to protect, betraying the trust that God had placed in him, he began to think that his appearance or glory could compete with the glory of God.

    Even to this day he tempts mankind, especially women, to do the same thing. As the cycle of role reversal continues to spin, even men are getting caught up in this destructive spirit of vanity. Honestly ask yourself, "Why do we battle with cut hair, dyed hair, make-up, fingernail polish, jewelry, and improper clothing?" We value our appearance; therefore, we want to do all in our power to enhance it. Focusing on the desire to be beautiful will corrupt our wisdom, and we will begin to value the paltry things of this world above our relationship with our Lord and Master, Jesus Christ.

If the Lucifer spirit has taken up residence in our hearts, it will cause us to rebel. We will oppose the preacher of righteousness who proclaims the Word of God when he admonishes us to remove the trappings of the world and to live a life of holiness. If we begin to value our appearance above the law of God, spiritual anarchy will be born in our hearts.

As a teenager, my mother decided to try a bit of clear fingernail polish on her nails. After she got all fixed up, she began to get caught up in admiring her shiny nails as she played the piano. When her father, A. D. Urshan, came into the room, he asked her what she had on her nails. Recognizing the spirit of vanity that wanted to overtake his daughter, that old pioneer of the faith quickly nipped it in the bud. He said that if God wanted her to have shiny nails, He would have given them to her. When Grandpa Urshan told mother to take it off, she immediately obeyed. But how many times, when the man of God begins to come against that spirit of vanity, do we want to rise in defense of that unclean spirit?

God commands the woman not to usurp authority over the man in I Timothy 2:12, ***"But I suffer not a woman to teach, nor to usurp authority over the man, but to be in silence."*** This Scripture has long been misunderstood and has been interpreted as saying that women are not allowed to speak in a church setting. If you examine the context in which it is written, Paul is referring to the marital relationship going all the way back to the first husband and wife, Adam and Eve. When a woman desires the things of the world, she can manipulate her husband to accept her desires for worldliness in things such as cutting her hair and wearing make-up and jewelry. Using her power of persuasion over her own husband, she bends him to her wishes. Then she has usurped his authority, and there is no holiness in her heart as it is now inhabited by the spirit of vanity. Like Adam, the man is placed in a difficult position; he now must choose between the will of God and the will of his wife. A woman must be careful that she does not influence her husband to turn away from holiness standards even if she does not want to obey them.

This a clear indication that another spirit has taken up residence in our hearts; no longer is the spirit of holiness in control.

We started a home missions church in Rio Rancho, New Mexico. We went from our living room to a storefront to our own building. One day in the storefront, a new family came to visit. When you have just a handful of people, that is quite an exciting occurrence. They dropped a fifty-dollar check in the offering box. That made things even more exciting. Little did we know that God was setting us up for a test and a learning experience.

They continued to come, dropping their fifty-dollar check in the box each time. After attending for a while, the wife approached us after church and asked about what we believed. My husband began to talk about the salvation message, but that was not her inquiry. Pointblank she asked us, "What about dresses, no make-up, and the 'buns' that I see on all the women?" God was testing our hearts to see if we would place our desire for success above obedience to Him. After all, is not the inordinate desire for success also founded in the spirit of vanity? We want others to perceive us as people who have really attained and who have it all together. We want to be successful, and a large church is perceived as success. My husband counted the cost and then began to wade into the explanation of holiness.

This was a family that was in role reversal and totally out of creation order. The husband stood behind her like a little lap dog, waiting to see what verdict she would cast concerning this church. She had completely usurped his authority, and it became very evident as the discussion progressed. She asked about the dresses, and we answered her. Her husband wagged his head in agreement, saying that he liked to see women in dresses. Next she asked about the "buns."

(Allow me to digress here a moment and shine the spotlight on the enemy's intimidation tactic. He refers to our glorious long hair as "buns." We don't wear "buns"; we wear "hairdos." But we will see in a moment just why he hates our hair so much. Now, back to the story.)

We told her why we wore long hair, and once again the husband voiced his opinion that he liked long hair on women. Finally, she asked about make-up. When we finished explaining, she looked us squarely in the eye and said, "I might consider wearing dresses and having the long hair, but I could never give up my make-up!" With that they left, the browbeaten husband scurrying after his domineering wife. What a tragic decision! She forfeited the opportunity for salvation for herself and for her family because of her desire for a pot of greasepaint and the bondage of vanity.

The spirit of vanity is so strong that it will persuade women to part with the promise of eternal life when they are under its influence. Their wisdom or sense of reason is corrupted. Their thinking becomes convoluted, causing them to think that worldly adornments are more valuable than the Kingdom of God. They will sacrifice their family's chance for salvation because of its influence. Time and time again we have families start to attend church, and the wife will look around and decide that holiness is not for her. Because her rebellion against God is rooted in vanity, she usurps authority and drags out her entire family with her.

This spirit can be even more disastrous if it takes a hold on a pastor's wife. It may ruin an entire congregation. This happened in a church with which I was very familiar.

The wife had always had a desire for the trappings of the world. It stayed hidden for a while until a root of bitterness took hold in the husband's life. She began to feed the spirit of bitterness and manipulated her husband. His thinking became so twisted that he began to let go of all the things that had been passed down to him. I had a rare occasion a few years past to go shopping with this pastor's wife, and I was heartbroken as I watched her buy the attire of the world unashamed in front of me. I ran from that spirit as fast as I could. Now the whole congregation that they pastor has been totally contaminated with the spirit of vanity and worldliness.

The enemy can use lay women to corrupt an entire assembly in a similar fashion. I watched some very domineering women in a church who desired to engage in all the fashions of Egypt. They also had quite a bit of money and were a ruling family in the church. One of them actually withstood the pastor to his face and told him to leave. They refused to give up until they found just the pastor they wanted, one who would tell them everything they wanted to hear and would let them do anything they wanted. This church finally pulled out of the UPCI and has become interdenominational. Anything goes there, and it all happened because of controlling women who were out of proper order and usurped authority. They persisted until they heaped to themselves teachers, having itching ears.

We are warned in I John 2:15-17 to *"Love not the world, neither the things that are in the world. If any man love the world, the love of the Father is not in him. For all that is in the world, the lust of the flesh, and the lust of the eyes, and the pride of life, is not of the Father, but is of the world. And the world passeth away, and the lust thereof: BUT HE THAT DOETH THE WILL OF GOD ABIDETH FOR EVER."* If we love anything more than Him, then we are not worthy of Him. In the last days, the Lord is walking throughout His Church, examining hearts. As He searches for those who are willing to forsake all to follow Him, one of the major tests that He is using is the test of holiness. How much do we really love Him? If we love the world, the love of the Father is not in us. If the pathway you are walking has begun to look suspiciously broad, if you look around and you do not look any different from the world that surrounds you, you better start examining your heart. What means more to you–your appearance or your relationship with the Father?

We need to understand that living a life of holiness and separation does not necessitate our becoming unkempt and ill smelling. Being sloppy does not equal being holy and does not glorify God any more than being worldly will. We are ambassadors of Christ, epistles known and read of all men. We should be a reflection of our royal Father and the mighty Kingdom that we represent. If you were to put a well-dressed, well-groomed woman of God in a room full of Egypt's women, she would outshine all of them in beauty and class. They would look at her in puzzlement, trying to figure out why she is so beautiful without all the trappings of the world. This is the beauty of holiness in all of its glory. God is a God of beauty and order. Psalm 50:2 says, **"Out of Zion, the perfection of beauty, God hath shined."** The Church is the perfection of beauty in this sinful world because the splendor of the Lord rests upon us. Proverbs 31 describes the godly woman as being well dressed. It is not a sin to look nice. The sin comes in when we want to disobey God's laws in order to enhance our outer appearance in ways that are contrary to His commands. We are to dress in a manner that becometh or is suitable and attractive for women professing godliness.

Once again let us consider the significance of the covering in connection with the glory of God. Ezekiel 28:14 and 16 states, *"Thou art the <u>anointed cherub that covereth</u>; and I have set thee so: thou wast upon the holy mountain of God; thou hast walked up and down in the midst of the stones of fire. By the multitude of thy merchandise they have filled the midst of thee with violence, and thou hast sinned: therefore I will cast thee as profane out of the mountain of God: and I will destroy thee, <u>O covering cherub</u>, from the midst of the stones of fire."* Lucifer's main responsibility was as the covering cherub that guarded the glory of God. When he was cast out, he lost his covering. God in His amazing and poetic nature delegated Lucifer's lost estate to the woman. *"For this cause ought the woman to have power on her head because of the angels. But if a woman have long hair, it is a <u>GLORY</u> to her: <u>for her hair is given her for a COVERING</u>"* (I Corinthians 11:10 and 15). This issue of the hair is of major proportions. The enemy tempts women over and over to tamper with the covering because it symbolizes to him everything he lost. When he sees a saint of God who is a guardian of the glory, he gnashes his teeth in frustration and anger. This is one of the sources of that enmity that God declared would be between the woman and the serpent in Genesis 3:15. Women are now the "Guardians of the Glory." As the aforementioned Scripture declares, it is a glory to the woman. The glory is not hers but is the glory of God residing upon her and in her life.

A woman's hair signals to the spirit world whether she is in rebellion or in submission. Is she in her correct place in God's order? The angels can tell by looking at her. There are two types of angels–the angels of the Lord and the angels of Lucifer. The woman's hair displays the influence that controls her life. What is one of the first things a woman does when she backslides? She attacks her head. She removes the glory. She loses her covering just like Lucifer lost his when he was cast out. No longer is she a guardian of the glory, for she has rebelled just like he did. She is now separated from God just like he is.

The only other place where you see these three components mentioned together–the covering, the angels, and the glory–is in the Ark of the Covenant. The mercy seat covered the testimony, the law. The cherubim, the angels assigned to guard the glory, covered the mercy seat and, indeed, were attached to it. Dwelling in the midst of the cherubim was the glory of God. If ever the covering, the mercy seat, was removed from the Ark, the angels were removed with it. They were attached to the covering. The glory, mercy, and presence of God were removed as well, leaving only naked law, no mercy. To forfeit the covering was to forfeit the divine protection!

The token of our New Testament salvation is the blood applied through baptism in Jesus' Name. Without the covering of the blood, we are exposed to naked law without mercy. The woman's hair is a type and shadow of the covering that Jesus provided for His Church. Not submitting to typology can be disastrous. (Just ask Moses.)

The woman, as God created her, is a picture of the Church–the Law on the inside; the covering of her submission to that law on the outside; the mercy and the angels covering her; and the glory and the presence of God dwelling over, around, and in the midst of her! The woman's uncut hair is a part of what makes her visible and recognizable as the covered bride of Jesus Christ.

Power Before The Throne

    Herein lies a fantastic promise of protection not only for the woman but also for her family. Ezekiel 10 with all its mystery surely indicates that wherever the glory was, the cherubim were as well. In verses 18 and 19, when the glory of the Lord departed from the house or the temple, the cherubim lifted up their wings and departed also. They were committed to the glory! We are the temple of the Holy Ghost, and the glory is in residence as long as our submission and place in the creation order are maintained through obedience and uncut hair. When a woman cuts her hair, she actually severs the glory of God from her life. The angels will lift and depart, for they are committed to the glory. Where there is no glory, the angels are absent except for judgment.

    Have you ever noticed that the armor of God does not make any provision for the back? For years I've heard it taught that this is because we are not supposed to turn our backs on the enemy. But God didn't leave us without protection for our backs. Isaiah 58:8 says that the glory of the Lord shall be our REARGUARD! Titus 2:5 says that women are to be "keepers at home." This phrase in the Greek language has a much deeper meaning than simply housekeeping (cooking, cleaning, etc.). It also means "a guard, to beware." Ladies, your job description involves more than housekeeping. You are to be a guard that will beware of any evil that would try to come into your homes.

We can actually open our homes for evil spirits to come in if we are in rebellion. Your uncut hair brings protection to the entire family. My sister related a story to me of a young minister's wife in the Dominican Republic. Her husband was a very promising young man in the Bible School, an exceptional preacher. My sister and husband consistently taught on holiness in the Bible School and throughout the work there. This young woman had long hair, but she persisted in trimming it despite what was taught. She opened her home for an invasion of the enemy because she lifted the covering through her disobedience. Before long her husband fell into adultery with a girl in their neighborhood. Their lives were shattered, and their ministry was completely ruined. The spirit of vanity had caused her to become more concerned about the appearance of her split ends than about her obedience to God.

Proverbs 31:11-12 says, ***"The heart of her husband doth safely trust in her, so that he shall have no need of***

spoil. She will do him good and not evil all the days of her life. " Can our husbands' hearts safely trust in us to guard the glory and to insure divine protection for our family so that no wicked spirit can enter in to spoil us? What an awesome responsibility, yet what a tremendous privilege that God has entrusted to the woman. He has placed a great deal of confidence in us. I admonish you; please, before you ever consider putting scissors to your hair, ask yourself, "Why am I doing this?" and "How will this affect my family?" Do you dare forfeit divine protection for the sake of vanity? Can the Lord depend on you to guard the glory faithfully and diligently?

*"**You were in Eden, the garden of God; every precious stone adorned you: ruby, topaz, and emerald, chrysolite, onyx and jasper, sapphire, turquoise and beryl. Your settings and mountings were made of gold; on the day you were created they were prepared**"* (Ezekiel 28:13 taken from the NIV translation).

One of the things that contributed to Lucifer's vanity was the covering of precious stones that he was created with. This helps us understand more clearly why the apostles stipulated in I Timothy 2:9 and I Peter 3:3 that we are not to adorn ourselves with gold and pearls. The Lord knew that the wearing of these things can promote the spirit of vanity in us and possibly make us become a traitor to the glory even as Lucifer did.

I came across an interesting bit of information in an article on pearls that was published by the American Gem Society. It sheds further light on the culture of Paul's day and why he particularly focused on the wearing of pearls. The article says, "The pearl was the favored gem of the wealthy during the time of the Roman Empire. Roman women wore pearls to bed so they could be reminded of their wealth immediately upon awakening." When Paul forbade the wearing of pearls, he was dealing with the spirit of vanity, which they promoted.

We have something far more valuable than gold or precious stones. We have been afforded the privilege of angelic protection and also a special place of ministry in God's kingdom. If we were to indulge a desire to wear jewelry, most of us could not afford the real thing and would have to settle for a cheap imitation. Is not our salvation worth more than a few inferior Egyptian baubles? Why yearn for that when God is going to give us streets of gold, gates of pearl, foundations comprised of all manner of precious stones, and, above all, eternal life that will be spent basking in the presence of the One we love more than anything else? Or do we love Him more than anything else? Our choices reveal what we value most.

What a comfort it is to know that the angels of the Lord are encamping around about our families, diligently on guard against any intrusion of the enemy forces. I cannot always be with my children twenty-four hours a day, but each day I send them off to school, pleading the blood of Jesus over them, praying the armor of God on them, and asking for the angels of the Lord to encamp around about them. We can ask this with confidence if we are in obedience to God's Word and have not severed the glory in our lives.

We can understand more clearly why God placed the wife under the protection of her husband in His creation order. Husbands are put there as a safeguard for the woman as she carries out this wondrously important duty that God has entrusted in her hands. God does not want women to make the same mistake that Eve did and to allow the enemy to make inroads into their families. Submission is the key to effectively guarding the glory and insuring divine protection for your family.

Only eternity will reveal how many times your family was protected because of this promise of power on your head. Bro. Mangus related a story to my sister about a precious saint of God that claimed this promise at a very desperate time in her life. This lady's son was in a very serious car accident. When he was brought into the emergency room, the doctors did not even work on him because they said he was too far gone. They left to go work on other patients that they thought had a better chance of survival. Somehow, this frantic mother managed to get into her son's room along with her husband. As she stood at his bedside, she began to pray. She reminded God of how a scissors had never touched her hair. She prayed the promise of I Corinthians 11:10 and claimed the power that was available to her because of the angels. God heard that prayer, and, immediately, things began to happen. The doctors came back, expecting to see a young man who possibly was dead. Instead, they found that he had regained consciousness and was responding. Within a matter of days, this young man was out of the hospital. His mother had guarded the glory, and she had power on her head because of the angels!

There are times when this power is at work on our behalf when we are not even aware of it. My friend, Steve Richardson, related the following incident to me that took place in his life. He had a very godly mother who never cut her hair and who was a woman of prayer. One day while driving on Highway 465 in Indianapolis, Indiana, Steve exited onto an overpass. There was a semitrailer and tractor truck stopped directly in front of him with a car underneath it. There had been an awful accident. Steve slammed on his brakes, and his car began to fishtail but did not slow down. Miraculously, his car went up on its left side between the semi and the concrete abutment. Even though there was no lane there, he came out safely on the other side. To this day Steve does not know how it happened. He should have been dead. Another truck driver told him that it literally looked like an angel picked up his car and set it down in a safe place. That angelic power was at work for Steve at a time when he was in a life or death situation. Thank God that his mother guarded the glory and that she had power on her head because of the angels.

Guardians Of The Glory

We never know when we are going to need that power.

I heard Bro. Stoneking relate a story about a woman who was in her house when she heard a scream. She ran outside and saw her child standing in the grass. Standing on the sidewalk was a woman actually trembling all over. She said, "You had left the window open, and your child climbed out on the window ledge. He fell down two stories, but there was a man standing there who caught him. The man has disappeared; I do not know where he went." This mother had power on her head because of the angels.

Ezekiel 10:12 describes the cherubim, the special guardian angels. It says that they are full of eyes. Their whole bodies, backs, hands, wings, and wheels are full of eyes. They are the watchers, and they see everything. Nothing can sneak up on them, and, consequently, we are protected round about. ***"The angel of the LORD encampeth round about them that fear him, and delivereth them"*** (Psalm 34:7). They are ministering spirits sent forth to minister on the behalf of the heirs of salvation. We must never sacrifice our inheritance rights for the sake of vanity and temporary indulgence in Egypt's fleshpots.

Proverbs 4:26-27 admonishes us with these words,

"Ponder the path of thy feet, and let all thy ways be established. Turn not to the right hand nor to the left: remove thy foot from evil." As saints of the Most High God, we must constantly guard against the spirit of delusion that would try to come against the Church. We must examine our motives and remove our foot from evil. The Word of God discerns our hearts by how we interpret it. I reflect on how God tested us in the storefront with the family previously mentioned. We may have lost a fifty-dollar check, but we have been given benefits far above that from the gracious hand of the Lord. Thank God that we did not desecrate the goodly heritage that has been passed on to us.

Isaiah 35 talks of the mighty outpouring that we all long for so desperately in these last days. As it details the mighty miracles that will take place and the spiritual blessings that will be poured out, the prophet of God stops to remind us that *"an highway shall be there, and a way, and it shall be called __THE WAY OF HOLINESS__; the __unclean__ shall not pass over it; but it shall be for those: the wayfaring men, though fools, shall not err therein"* (Isaiah 35:8). The highway that leads to end time revival and the resulting harvest is not the broad, wide way of compromise, but it is the strait and narrow way called "the highway of holiness." We are further instructed in Isaiah 62:10, *"Go through, go through the gates; prepare ye the way of the people; cast up, cast up the highway; gather out the stones; lift up a standard for the people."* Let us build up the highway of holiness, gathering out the stones, the things that we have stumbled over, and lifting up a standard for the people. Let us lift the banner high, proclaiming holiness with a loud voice. God is coming back for a glorious church which has not severed the glory from her head but has maintained diligent protection of it.

If we stay on the pathway of righteousness and allow the Word of God to continue to shine the spotlight of truth upon our motives, we will be kept from the spirit of vanity and strong delusion. Paul warns us in II Thessalonians 2:11-12 that strong delusion is sent and people begin to believe lies, which result in damnation, when they have "pleasure in unrighteousness." Lord, help us to guard the glory with our very lives and keep that which you have committed unto us. Let us never value anything above our Lord, our relationship with Him, and obedience to His

Word. May we walk worthy unto all pleasing before the One who has delivered us from the power of darkness and has translated us into the Kingdom of His dear Son!

"Search me, O God, and know my heart: try me, and know my thoughts: And see if there be any wicked way in me, and lead me in the way everlasting" (Psalm 139:23-24).

Naboth refused to give his inheritance to Ahab. He was not for sale. His inheritance meant more to him than money or prestige. Are you for sale? Can the enemy buy you with promises of success and temporary prominence? Is he drawing you in with the deceitfulness of his fashion agenda in which he strips away all your God-given beauty and then hands you a cheap cover-up? Lucifer is a merchandiser according to Ezekiel 28:16 and 18. He will try to strike a deal with you and prevail on you to sell your inheritance. He will make promises of bigger and better vineyards if you will only fall down and worship him, but we must never sell out and become a traitor to our heritage! *". . . It is written, Thou shalt worship the Lord thy God, and him only shalt thou serve"* (Matthew 4:10).

God, give us men and women of God who are not

for sale–those who will guard the glory and pass it down from generation to generation! If we sell our inheritance for our appearance, a larger church, or to increase our fame and fortune, the spirit of vanity that destroyed Lucifer has arrived. The enemy tells us that this is a new era and that we need to let go of our inheritance to fill our churches; however, we must not be deceived by his lies. Our morality will dictate our theology. There is a difference between growing and swelling. A church may swell because of infection brought on by the absence of holiness, but true growth can only be achieved in a church that is spiritually healthy. Let us keep the infection of compromise from invading our lives and churches. **We must be guardians of the glory!**

Power Before The Throne

Power Before The Throne

Come and walk with me, if you will, through the intriguing and inspiring story of Esther as we examine the inner workings of the battle that was fought between good and evil, between light and darkness. As the story unfolds, we see . . .

* * * * * * * * * *

Pompously, Haman strutted through the streets of Shushan. His heart swelled with pride and delight as one by one the people bowed low before him and did obeisance. Was he not Haman, the Agagite and a descendant of the royal house of Agag, who was once a mighty king of the Amalekites? He deserved the place of honor that King

Power Before The Throne

Ahasuerus had bestowed upon him, and he intended to enjoy it to the full. As he surveyed the crowd of bowing subjects, his eye fell upon a lone figure standing tall and unabashed amongst the prostrate forms around him. Haman's eyes narrowed, and his face contorted with anger. How dare this man defy the king's commandment?

Mordecai stared back unflinchingly and remained conspicuously upright even as those around him pulled on his robe and bade him to bow. He would not make peace with an enemy of God, neither would he compromise in the midst of a heathen society where he was a stranger. After all, the reason Israel had been removed to a foreign land in the first place was because she had embraced the idolatrous ways of the heathen that surrounded her. But this son of Abraham had pledged his loyalty and devotion to none else but the great El Shaddai. Nothing could persuade him to bow the knee. Only One was worthy of that kind of adoration.

Furiously, Haman gathered his silken, purple robes around him and stormed into his palatial residence. Assembling his servants, he made vigorous inquiry as to the identity of this defiant upstart who refused to bow before him. The information was quickly relayed that Mordecai was a Jew. The Jews had their own special code of conduct that superseded the laws of man. Fawning over Haman, the informants told of how they had admonished Mordecai over and over to bow the knee to Haman. Mordecai disdained their counsel, refusing to comply with this command.

As Haman pondered the information, he thought back to the age-old feud that existed between the Amalekites and the Israelites. Then and there, he determined he would not stop with the destruction of just one man, but he would destroy the entire nation of the Jews. Never again would another of those obnoxious people mar his glory and prestige in the kingdom or fight against any remaining Amalekites. Ah, yes, it would take place in the month Adar. One year from now all his enemies would be annihilated.

Haman approached King Ahasuerus with his request and waited as the King pondered the advice that had been laid out for his consideration. After deliberating for a moment, the King pulled off his signet ring and handed it to Haman. Looking fondly as his chief prince, the King granted him permission to use whatever resources were needed to protect the interests of the kingdom.

Leaving the King's presence, Haman had a difficult time keeping his jubilation to himself. It had all been so easy. Feeling like dancing, he quickly dispatched the news throughout the kingdom. Soon, Mordecai and his people would be history.

When Mordecai perceived all that Haman intended to do, he threw off his elegant palace garb and donned sackcloth. He sprinkled ashes over himself and cried loudly and bitterly as he entered the open square before the King's gate. There was a special emissary located in the house of the King who had been placed there by the majestic hand of the Almighty for such a time as this. She was someone who had power before the throne.

Hearing the commotion in the street, Queen Esther quickly ran to her window to peer out. To her amazement, there was a man covered in sackcloth and ashes. It was totally contrary to the law to enter the gate of the King dressed in such a fashion, and he was getting dangerously close to the entrance. As she stared, the man turned his face toward her window. It could not be! Surely this was not Mordecai; such a disturbance could cost him his life. She sent proper clothing to Mordecai, but he refused to take the royal attire offered to him.

She urgently dispatched her attendant Hatach to question Mordecai as to the reason for his strange behavior. Hatach returned with a copy of the King's decree, which declared that all the Jews would be killed. It was accompanied by a chilling request from her beloved cousin. He charged her to make supplication before the King for the life of her people. The time had come to reveal her true identity which had long been kept secret.

She sent back a message to Mordecai, reminding him that she could not casually appear before the King when it pleased her. The King had not summoned her for thirty days; should she appear before him unannounced and he did not extend the royal scepter, she would pay for such an intrusion with her life.

Mordecai responded with the same uncompromising advice. If she held her peace, deliverance would arise from some other place, but she and her father's house would be destroyed. He closed his plea with a final thought provoking word, "... **Who knoweth whether thou art come to** *the kingdom for such a time as this?"* (Esther 4:14).

After considering the words of her cousin, Esther returned her answer to Mordecai, *"Go, gather together all the Jews that are present in Shushan, and fast ye for me, and neither eat nor drink three days, night or day: I also and my maidens will fast likewise; and so will I go in unto the king, which is not according to the law: and if I perish, I perish"* (Esther 4:16).

Esther awoke before dawn on the third day of her proclaimed fast. As she pondered what course of action to take, an ingenious plan formulated in her mind. She began to search through her royal wardrobe, looking for the dress that had captured the King's attention and affection the first time they met. There it was.

Knowing that her beauty must capture the King's attention, Esther called for her maids to help her prepare for the unexpected appearance in the royal court. Finally, she was ready. Looking in the mirror, she was pleased to see her graceful elegance and beauty was enhanced to the fullest. She took a deep breath, said farewell to her handmaidens, and ventured toward the forbidden precincts of the royal court.

Power Before The Throne

Standing in the inner court, she could see the King sitting upon his throne, clothed in his regal robe with a crown upon his head. As their eyes met, her breath caught in her throat, and her heart pounded furiously. This was it, the moment of destiny. Her life and the life of her people hung in the balance. Slowly, the seconds ticked by as her fate was being decided. Taken back to the first time he had seen his beloved Esther, the King's mouth turned up in a brilliant smile. His hand tightened on his scepter as he raised it to signify the acceptance of his bride in the royal court. Touching the scepter, Esther graciously petitioned for His Royal Majesty, along with the chief prince, Haman, to be present at a banquet she was preparing that very afternoon. He accepted with delight.

The King summoned Haman, and together they feasted on the finest delicacies that the kingdom of Persia had to offer. Enjoying Esther's pleasant hospitality, the King once again inquired as to her request. She countered with one more banquet invitation, promising to reveal all on the morrow.

As soon as the King and Haman departed, Esther and her household began intense preparations for the final stage of her God-ordained plan. Meanwhile, Haman joyfully made his way home. Haman called together his wife and friends, recounting all the grand things that had befallen him that day. Tomorrow he would be the only honored guest at a private banquet with the King and Queen. But none of this mattered as long as that upstart named Mordecai refused to bow down to him. His friends suggested that a gallows be built to hang Mordecai so that Haman could go to the banquet tomorrow with a merry heart. "What an excellent idea," thought Haman, summoning the carpenters. The gallows would be finished by tomorrow. That would be the perfect time to obtain permission from the King to put Mordecai to death.

Haman's murderous conspiracy was doomed to failure. Haman began to fall headlong into the pit of destruction that he had dug for someone else. Behind the scenes in the spiritual realm, light began to triumph over darkness. Soon, Haman would hang on his own gallows; Mordecai would become the prince of the land; and the people of God would be granted power over their adversaries.

Power Before The Throne

* * * * * * * * * *

As the final drama between good and evil unfolds, the Church needs men like Mordecai who refuse to bow to the prince of this world. We need women who are unashamed of their godly heritage, refusing to compromise in a hostile environment of role reversal, feminism, and licentious living.

The paradox will never change–victory over the enemy and his ultimate destruction will always come by way of submission to the cross and death to self. God has placed some Mordecais and Esthers in strategic places for such a time as this, holy men and women who will never bow to this world. We must never abdicate our power before the throne!

"For this cause ought the woman to have power on her head because of the angels" (I Corinthians 11:10). The Greek word for "power" is **exousia** (pronounced *ex-oo-'see-ah*). It means "privilege, force, capacity, competency, freedom, mastery, delegated influence or authority, liberty." Contrary to some heretical beliefs which have been circulating, this delegated power allows women freedom to remain in obedience to God's commands. This does not place them in slavery but, instead, frees them from the dangerous consequences that can result from their rebellion and unwillingness to submit. In these last days, as we wage war against the forces of darkness, we need to have a proper perspective of the tremendous advantage afforded to the Church.

In Genesis 3:15, God decreed that there would be enmity between the serpent and the woman. God promised victory to the woman and gave her the key in verse sixteen. *"... And thy desire shall be to thy husband, and he shall rule over thee."* Victory comes as a result of a woman's submission to her husband. When a woman submits to her husband and exhibits that submission through her uncut hair, the power of God is loosed on her behalf, thereby defeating the enemy that would try to destroy her family. It was Esther's submission to Mordecai that brought salvation not only to her nation but also, ultimately, to her family. When the Church is in submission to her husband, the Lord Jesus Christ, and exhibits her submission through obedience to God's command for holiness, the destruction of the enemy is insured.

Power Before The Throne

Psalm 11:3 says, ***"If the foundations be destroyed, what can the righteous do?"*** The foundations of our society have been eroded, the gender roles have become blurred, and every man is doing that which is right in his own eyes. As the righteous seed of the Kingdom, we do not have to wring our hands in panicked futility. We have power before the throne! We must lift up a standard against the flood of wickedness pervading the land.

The devil realizes the power the Church has at its disposal. Having once enjoyed the same delegated authority before the throne, he feverishly tries to take it from us. If he can persuade us to become tolerant of worldliness, we will be no different from the helpless victims who surround us on every side. He wants the Church to lose spiritual mastery over his kingdom, enabling him to take us captive at his will. If we lay our head in Delilah's lap (the lap of wickedness), we will awaken and shake ourselves only to find our strength was removed when the glory was severed.

Paul exhorts us in Romans 16:17-20, ***"Now I beseech you, brethren, mark them which cause divisions and offences contrary to the doctrine which ye have learned; and avoid them. For they that are such serve*** *not our Lord Jesus Christ, but their own belly; and by good works and fair speeches deceive the hearts of the simple. For <u>your obedience</u> is come abroad unto all men. I am glad therefore on your behalf: but yet I would have you wise unto that which is good, and simple concerning evil. <u>And the God of peace shall bruise Satan under your feet shortly.</u> The grace of our Lord Jesus Christ be with you. Amen."* At the beginning of the book of Esther, Haman was writing the decrees, but at the end the power had been transferred to Mordecai and Esther. A Church that refuses to bow will be empowered to finalize the destruction of Satan. Even as Mordecai waxed greater and greater, becoming second in command in the kingdom of Persia and dwelling in the house of his archenemy, God's Church is going to wax greater and greater until the day we rule and reign with our Lord over the kingdoms of this world.

I close with the triumphant promise set forth in Isaiah 60:1-3. It says, *"ARISE, SHINE; for thy light is come, and the <u>glory of the LORD</u> is risen upon thee. For, behold, the darkness shall cover the earth, and gross darkness the people: but the LORD shall arise upon thee,* *and **his glory shall be seen upon thee**. And the Gentiles shall come to thy light, and kings to the brightness of thy rising."* Today is a day of gross darkness upon the earth: a day when they call good evil and evil good. Truth lies fallen in the streets; sin abounds more and more. However, during this time, God's glory will arise upon His Church. We talk about end time revival and the resulting harvest; we preach about it and pray for it; nevertheless, it will be given to the people who visibly show forth His glory. The Church that shines forth as a beacon of glory, a people who refuse to bow to the prince of this world, is come to the Kingdom for such a time as this. We have POWER BEFORE THE THRONE!